Anger Therapy

Anger Therapy

written by
**Lisa O. Engelhardt and
Karen Katafiasz**

illustrated by
R.W. Alley

**ONE
CARING
PLACE**

Abbey Press

Text © 1995 Karen Katafiasz and Lisa O. Engelhardt
Illustrations © 1995 St. Meinrad Archabbey
Published by One Caring Place
Abbey Press
St. Meinrad, Indiana 47577

Library of Congress Catalog Number
95-79169

ISBN 978-0-87029-292-7

Printed in the United States of America

Foreword

Anger is a painful, powerful, and complex emotion. When it overwhelms your spirit, you may at first just want to push it away or stuff it down, as you try to ignore or forget it.

Or you may look for a quick and easy release, no matter how unfocused your feelings, how inappropriate the situation, or how undeserving the target of your rage—as long as you can discharge the terrible feeling inside you.

But not dealing effectively with your anger only increases its potential to be destructive.

With clear and compelling guidelines, *Anger Therapy* leads you through the steps of acknowledging your anger, identifying its cause, determining what you can do, expressing your feelings, and taking any necessary action. It invites you to use your anger to learn about yourself and to turn that anger into energy for positive change.

Anger doesn't have to leave you feeling helpless, defeated, and immobile. With *Anger Therapy*, you can —as the book suggests—"love your anger....It has helped to sculpt the beauty of your soul."

1.

Anger is God's gift, part of the essence of your humanity, a response you need to survive and to thrive physically and emotionally. Use your anger to protect and preserve your true self.

2.

Anger is a signal—that your rights have been violated, your needs aren't being met, you're compromising yourself in some way, an injustice has been done. Let anger be a catalyst to learn more about yourself and create change for the better.

3.

You can turn the pain of anger into energy for change with five steps: Acknowledge your anger, identify its cause, determine what you can do, express your feelings judiciously, and, if necessary, take action.

4.

You may have learned to avoid, deny, or repress your anger because disturbing emotions can accompany it: You feel "bad," childish, insecure, powerless; you believe you'll be disliked and rejected; you fear being out of control. Accept your anger as an emotional fact—and a tool you can use for personal transformation.

5.

Anger that you lock inside can lodge in body cells and tissues, organs and systems—causing headaches, muscle tension, digestive disorders, high blood pressure, insomnia, and other physical problems. Be good to your body by acknowledging and dealing with your anger.

6.

Anger can come in different disguises or be an unseen facet of other emotions, like depression, grief, irritability, anxiety, hatred, guilt, shame, withdrawal, or resentment. And sometimes those emotions can show up as anger. Take time to sift through your moods and feelings to discover any hidden anger.

7.

Identify the trigger for your anger; clarify what's happening. Are rights and boundaries—yours or another's—being violated? Are you compromising or losing yourself in some way? Are your needs, dreams, talents being ignored?

8.

In the process of identifying what's causing your anger, you determine what is and is not acceptable to you. This is vital self-knowledge. Use it to guide your choices and shape your life.

9.

Determine how you can change the situation that is causing your anger. Sometimes there's specific action you can take. Sometimes you can remove yourself from patterns of relating that generate anger. Sometimes all you can do is change your attitude. But you can always do something.

10.

Focus on what <u>you</u> can do that will decrease your anger. It may seem as if others are the problem: if only <u>they</u> would change… But you can't change others. People are not responsible for your anger, only for their actions. No one else can "make" you angry, and no one else can take your anger away.

11.

Like a laser, anger can be a potent force for destruction or healing, depending on how it is used. Anger misused can destroy relationships with sharp words, fiery explosions, and smoldering resentments. Used effectively, anger can cut surgically through emotional debris, allowing healing change to happen.

12.

When you're angry, your body responds with increased pulse, breathing, and blood pressure; muscles tense up; adrenaline is released. Don't try to defuse your anger with unrestrained ranting and yelling. Contrary to popular belief, it will only intensify your rage and physical responses. To calm your anger, you need to find a way to act effectively.

13.

If you feel as if you're going to explode in anger, channel your physical responses into harmless physical activity. Breathe deeply, run a mile, swing a tennis racket. Later, return to your anger and deal with it peacefully and productively.

14.

Venting your anger in a controlled way to a sympathetic listener can bring temporary relief. But venting in itself won't solve the underlying problems that are triggering your anger. Search for those problems and deal with them.

15.

When you're angry at others,
tell them directly what disturbs
you and why. Don't shame,
blame, attack, ridicule, lecture,
interpret or analyze their
behavior. Use "I" statements.
Be specific in your requests.

16.

When you're expressing your
anger to others, you don't need
to convince them that your
position is right. Listen with
empathy to their point of view.
Allow them to feel angry too
(without blaming yourself for
their anger). And then together
try to arrive at a creative
solution that meets the needs
of both of you.

17.

Expressing anger may be difficult if you were taught to soothe over conflicts or to defer to others' feelings. Recognize when these old lessons have you stuffing your anger. Pleasing others at your own expense is not kind or peaceful. It's violence to your own psyche.

18.

There will be times when expressing your anger will be extremely difficult and painful. The outcome may be uncertain; you may be risking great change in your relationship. But just as God gives you anger to protect yourself, God provides courage to take the action your anger demands. Your courage is within you; ask God to help you find it.

19.

Along with expressing your feelings, you may need to take further action to eliminate reasons for your anger. Determine what you can do: decide your priorities, change your behavior in a relationship, address your own unmet needs. Then do it.

20.

Changing a problem situation usually takes more than one confrontation with another or more than one instance of different behavior on your part. Be persistent.

21.

Don't act or attempt serious communication in the heat of anger. At this time, your strongest desire may be to retaliate and hurt others the way you've been hurt. And your communication will likely be ineffective and consequently rejected, which will only intensify your sense of injustice. Remember that anger itself is a reaction—and shouldn't be an action.

22.

Anger is at times so intense because it can be about past situations as much as—or even more than—the present. If your anger seems out of proportion to what apparently triggered it or if it never quite seems to go away, start looking backward. You may have accumulated layers of pushed-down, denied, ignored anger.

23.

Ask yourself if the way you now feel reminds you of how you felt before. Recall the circumstances that surrounded your past anger. Anger can open a door to the past, a door through which you can enter and bring healing to old, unresolved issues.

24.

As a child, you were probably not equipped to deal with your anger or even allowed to express it. Yet if you were abused or mistreated or your boundaries violated, if you were not allowed to fully be and express your unique self, then your spirit was broken. The anger you felt was a healthy response. Allow the child within you to remember and to experience that anger now.

25.

If you were shamed or rejected for your anger in childhood, those feelings may be closely intertwined with your anger now. Reflect back on those moments. Discard the shame, replacing it with an affirmation of your worth and goodness. Promise that you will never reject or abandon the hurting child within you.

26.

You can't change the past and you can't change those who abused you or make them sorry, if they choose not to be. Claim the power you do have. You can decide to express your anger to them now. If doing so would put you in a vulnerable or painful situation, you can decide not to.

27.

As an adult, you can choose to see those who hurt and abused you in childhood as flawed, unaware, wounded. You no longer depend on them for survival; you're not as vulnerable to their rejection. Let them be. And let your anger go.

28.

If your anger is deeply rooted, you may need professional guidance to deal with it. A counselor can help you remove the layers of unresolved anger and shame and lead you toward a clear sense of yourself as precious and worthy of love.

29.

Once you deal with your anger, you can turn your attention to forgiving. When you hold on to your resentment, you freeze yourself in a victim's role, freezing some of your emotional energy as well. Let the warmth of understanding and the awareness of your worth thaw your emotions.

30.

Listen nonjudgmentally and without fear to others' anger—including that of children. Respect and validate their anger, whether or not you agree with their issues. Their anger belongs to them and need not threaten you.

31.

You are not responsible for others' anger, only for your own actions. If you have inadvertently offended someone, apologize and do your part to make things right. If you have hurt someone intentionally, also explore the source of your own anger.

32.

The negative traits in others
that anger us are often those
that we reject in ourselves.
Bring your shadow side—
the impulses and weaknesses
that you hide from yourself
and others—into the light
of self-truth.

33.

Let your anger guide you to social as well as personal change. Defend the innocent, protect the weak, help the helpless. Advocate, vote, minister, volunteer, serve others. Turn your anger at injustice into energy for transforming the world.

34.

Human emotions are interconnected in a web of surpassing beauty and strength. If you suppress one emotion, like anger, you damage your total emotional well-being. Release and resolve your anger and you will release unbounded passion, energy, and joy.

35.

The anger that you have embraced has etched deep canyons of humility, compassion, courage, and strength within you. Love your anger; share the gifts it has given you. It has helped to sculpt the beauty of your soul.

36.

You can love your anger without living your anger. When you feel angry—as you will many times in your life—read over the steps in this book that apply. Then use your anger to become more yourself, more at peace, more alive.

Karen Katafiasz is a writer and editor. She is the author of *Finding Your Way Through Grief, Celebrate-your-womanhood Therapy, Grief Therapy, Christmas Therapy*, and *Self-esteem Therapy*. A native of Toledo, Ohio, she now lives in Santa Claus, Indiana.

Lisa O. Engelhardt is editorial director for One Caring Place/Publications at Abbey Press and the author of *Finding the Serenity of Acceptance, Acceptance Therapy*, and *Happy Birthday Therapy*. She lives with her husband and three children in Lawrenceburg, Indiana.

Illustrator for the Abbey Press Elf-help Books, **R.W. Alley** also illustrates and writes children's books. He lives in Barrington, Rhode Island, with his wife, daughter, and son.

The Story of the Abbey Press Elves

The engaging figures that populate the Abbey Press "elf-help" line of publications and products first appeared in 1987 on the pages of a small self-help book called *Be-good-to-yourself Therapy*. Shaped by the publishing staff's vision and defined in R.W. Alley's inventive illustrations, they lived out author Cherry Hartman's gentle, self-nurturing advice with charm, poignancy, and humor.

Reader response was so enthusiastic that more Elf-help Books were soon under way, a still-growing series that has inspired a line of related gift products.

The especially endearing character featured in the early books—sporting a cap with a mood-changing candle in its peak—has since been joined by a spirited female elf with flowers in her hair.

These two exuberant, sensitive, resourceful, kindhearted, lovable sprites, along with their lively elfin community, reveal what's truly important as they offer messages of joy and wonder, playfulness and co-creation, wholeness and serenity, the miracle of life and the mystery of God's love.

With wisdom and whimsy, these little creatures with long noses demonstrate the elf-help way to a rich and fulfilling life.

Elf-help Books

...adding "a little character" and a lot
of help to self-help reading!

Book price is $4.95 unless otherwise noted.
Available at your favorite gift shop or bookstore—
or directly from One Caring Place, Abbey Press
Publications, St. Meinrad, IN 47577.
Or call 1-800-325-2511.
www.carenotes.com